MW01275298

The Coming Age of Internetocracy

By Lawrence A. Compagna

First edition copyright 2011

Second edition (completely revised)

Copyright 2012

ISBN: 978-1-105-68389-3

Published by Lulu.com

This book is dedicated to that famous fellow who bravely stood before the tanks at Tiananmen Square

Too bad we don't know your name...

Acknowledgements

The author acknowledges the friends and family who graciously took the time to read, edit, and offer their candid opinions during the writing of this book; in particular the three generations of the Compagna family who all contributed: A.M. Compagna for her on-going support of the project, C. Compagna for acting as the "sounding board" for the ideas expressed in this document, W. Compagna for sharing his prowess with social networking, and M. Compagna for sharing her knowledge of publishing.

I also thank the political group "Partido de Internet" of Spain for translating this work into their language, as well as the many users of the Internetocracy Facebook page who offered their tremendously helpful insights and suggestions, many of which are incorporated into this book.

A special thanks to those online faithful who helped "crowd source" a constitution modeled on the principles in this book in the spring of 2012.

Table of Contents

Preface

A few months after this book was written a peculiar movement began... "Occupy Wall Street". At first the movement did not seem to have a defined purpose, but as time went on it became clear that many of the demands of the occupiers seemed to be compatible with those expressed in this book.

At the time of writing the second edition the movement continues to grow and where it ends I have no idea. See the afterword for more on this phenomenon and how it relates to Internetocracy.

One further item to mention before you read further. In this book, representative democracy is used a "catch all" term to denote any political system where the voting rights of the majority have been entrusted to a small elected group of representatives. This includes American style republics (discussed later in the book), Canadian style confederations, as well as federations, constitutional monarchies, etc. Also note that our focus throughout this book is the Federal level of government.

_____

You make the laws:

No political parties

No representatives

Just Internetocracy

facebook.com/internetocracy   Click "Like" to join

When Ideas Meet Gunfire

Flash forward to another place and time. The youth are rebelling. They face tanks; they face the armies of the people in power.

They have only rudimentary weapons, but they have a cause: they want to be empowered to make decisions on the issues raised in their parliament, their duma, their congress. They have grown weary of being "represented" by politicians when, thanks to the internet, they are able to represent themselves.

They are tired of a small segment of the population unduly influencing these political representatives in ways that benefit only them. They are tired of corporations paying lobbyists to influence these representatives for their benefit.

In short, each adult man and woman desires a way to influence the lawmaking bodies of the world directly, without the use of a representative.

It has finally dawned on the masses: the internet has developed such that they can become directly involved in the political process and that "Internetocracy" has become possible.

So they demonstrate peacefully, and when that does not work, the demonstrations become more aggressive, and when even that does not work the non-violent protests begin to take an ugly turn, especially when the peaceful demonstrations are met with violence.

The Coming Age of Internetocracy

To reiterate, no longer do the masses want to rely upon a "representative" who is often swayed by party policy, lobbyists, or personal greed. That is not to say there are some do-gooder politicians, but far too often even the do-gooder is representing their own view of what is good and not the view of his or her constituent.

***

The peaceful protesting dies out, but because their voices are not heard the protests turn violent. Thousands die, but the people in power hang on. They will not relinquish their power without a fight.

The change that is coming is inevitable, and also intolerable to the people in power.

Those two forces are about to collide in the coming years.

Thousands always die when a new political idea takes hold of the youth.   Think of the turmoil in the Middle East in 2011, or the French Revolution, or the Russian Revolution, or even the American Revolution.   The shift to a new and completely revolutionary political idea is seldom attained through peaceful means.   A class of people in power seldom give it up peacefully.

They all involved new political ideas that rattled the existing power base, and they all resulted in huge shifts in power, but not before thousands or even millions had died.

> **"THERE IS ONE THING STRONGER THAN EVERY ARMY IN THE WORLD, AND THAT IS AN IDEA WHOSE TIME HAS COME"** -
> VICTOR HUGO
>
> A MESSAGE FOR THE THINKING MAN
> BROUGHT TO YOU BY INTERNETOCRACY

The "Wave"

"A connected, motivated group can now accomplish tasks otherwise thought impossible, at speeds and scales that we are only beginning to understand." Larry Shaughnessy (CNN correspondent).

It will come.

The mere existence of the technology to facilitate it, and a population infinitely more educated than when democracy first took hold centuries ago, means that the movement will eventually rise up, and it will be opposed by the existing powers, and the power will be overcome by the new movement.

Unfortunately today's powerful people will not sit idly by, so the change will only come about with violence. But it will come.

I am:

☐ Republican

☐ Democrat

☑ Awake

A message from facebook.com/INTERNETOCRACY

Visit our page to learn about a new political ideology (and "Like" if you are interested)

The "Wave" described

What will come?   What is the "Wave" of which I speak?

The revolutionary idea of which I speak is that of ONE issue, ONE person, and ONE direct vote lodged on the internet with the expert assistance of special advisers who stay tightly connected with the world of his or her constituent using the social networking tools that have emerged over the past few years as well as sites such as YouTube to make frequent and direct broadcasts to the constituents. It also harnesses technology so that special advisers can spend more time in face-to-face town hall style meetings or even impromptu congresses advertised via twitter.

The following diagram is a simplified representation of such an "Internetocracy":

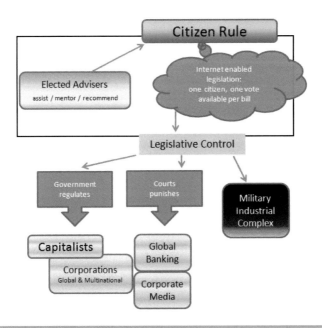

The Coming Age of Internetocracy

Contrast the previous diagram to this diagram of the present political, judicial, social, and economic landscape:

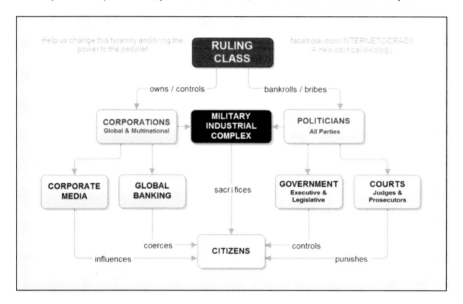

Some issues will seem quite simple to the voter and he or she will need very little assistance from the special adviser. Others are complex bills, perhaps a free trade bill or a bill to limit immigration. Such bills will rely heavily upon the advice of the special adviser to guide the people through the weighty issues.

Obviously the special adviser will still be a person of some prominence and wielding significant power, but those powers will be significantly less than elected officials have today. In a representative political system the elected official is in office for a period of time and can vote on a bill as he or she sees fit... often having to tow the party line or worse yet; succumbing to the lobbying influence of an unseen special interest group. More often than not these unseen lobbying groups are large corporations and the wealthy.

Furthermore, some representative political systems allow for significant campaign contributions that effectively make the elected official beholden to those who provided the funds to get them elected.

These abuses are limited in a new system where elected officials either do not exist or do not actually make the final decisions when it comes to legislation.

In today's representative political system we have one person who can elect one representative. This model, which was at one time revolutionary, has now become outdated. The old model was necessary because of the vast distances between the centers of power and the constituents.

Today's technology has made these distances irrelevant. With the internet comes the ability for every man and woman to study and vote on every issue. The only requirements are an internet enabled device, an internet connection and an ability to read and write.

The ability to read and write, at one time informally thought to be the minimum educational requirement to vote, will now have to be accompanied by another requirement. Everyone must have access to the internet.

The ability of every man and woman to propose legislation and vote on legislation they have an interest in via the internet with the support of special advisers who provide sage advice to their constituents will from this point on be called "Internetocracy".

How it Will Work

You sit down at your computer.   You have a cup of coffee next to the keyboard; it's a beautiful sunny day. You check your email, your Facebook, the news.

Now you log in to the voting portal.

The voting portal is a secure connection, just like the one you use for banking, but with a look and feel more akin to Facebook.

There are a handful of issues being considered by government right now. You are only interested in two of those, so you will not vote on the others. You will be considered as abstaining from those votes, and leaving the matters to others who wish to have a say.

It isn't necessary for everyone to be able to vote on every bill.   A small random sample of the population is all that is statistically necessary to tell with high accuracy what the whole population wants.

But the other two you are deeply interested in. One involves prison reform, and the other is a bill to change the speed limit from 70 miles per hour to 60.

You are not allowed to vote until you have studied the mandatory information. The mandatory information includes a summary of the issue, a summary of the proposal, and a written recommendation from your adviser. In addition to the mandatory documents there are other documents deemed optional.   Among the optional documents are detailed documents, statistics, studies, and even YouTube videos that provide a forum for both sides of the debate. The writings, videos, and other communications of your adviser will be critical in assisting the electorate to make wise decisions.

Because the political system is virtual, no longer requiring representatives to sequester themselves in the seat of power (Washington in the case of the USA for example), your adviser can spend far more time in the region they represent facilitating face-to-face town halls that are also streamed live on the internet.   At the federal level, the system would in fact foster more face-to-face meetings to discuss issues than the current representative form of government.

During town hall meetings suggestions could be streamed back to the town hall meeting so that those who could not attend in person still have input. Think of the constitution in Iceland that was recently "crowd sourced" in such a fashion.

To make it difficult for any single person to consolidate political power the regional adviser/mentor would represent a relatively small group of people from that region (I suggest a maximum of 1000 citizens) and would conduct town hall meetings relating to local, state/provincial, and federal legislation. You might attend some or all of these meetings, but you would not be required to.

Aside from the wise guidance of the special adviser, there are also user blogs on the subject, and a comments page. There is even a Facebook page you belong to where the issues are discussed via wall posts, notes, etc.

You read a few of these, but they too are optional.

Before voting you have just finished watching a very interesting YouTube video where the issue is hotly debated by both proponents and detractors.

There is also a video library on the website's server... And any face to face debates are recorded and placed in the video library. You can log in at any time and watch them. When you are ready to cast your vote, you can go in and cast it. You can do it right after you have done your mandatory research, or sleep on it, and then vote. Both are acceptable so long as the vote is cast within the permitted window. The voting window would span weeks, with the current status of the vote displayed as soon as the voting has opened. So as to avoid "groupthink" users would have no knowledge of the votes for and against until the vote has closed. Seeing the current direction of voting would impel some to vote with the majority, when they might have voted otherwise had they not have had such knowledge.

Reviewing these videos, blogs, and comments are optional, but the required documents are a minimum if one wishes to be eligible to vote on an issue.

You study these documents. They summarize the issue, and both sides of the argument.

You then go to an online forum where you can discuss the issue with other people who are interested in it. You interact with others real time. One person gives you their phone number and you call them to discuss. You discuss the issue with a friend over Skype.

All this took you an hour on a beautiful Saturday morning.

You've done your research, you feel ready to vote even though the deadline is not for another week. So you vote "Yes" to the prison reform bill, and "no" on the other issue.

You log off your account and head to another important function: Your date with a surfboard at the beach.

Tabling Legislation

So how did pending legislation get tabled?

Ideas for new legislation are "voted" on with a "Like" button, similar to what exists on Facebook. Anyone can suggest something, just like anyone with a user ID can create a Facebook page for any issue.   Advisers can also recommend ideas to be put forward for debate and the respect they hold in their region would likely help push their recommendations to nearer to the top of the list.

Even the selection of your adviser/mentor was simple. Just "Like" them as you would on Facebook. Until you unlike them they remain as your adviser/mentor, but you can only have one at a time. See the Leadership section for more information on this.

The look and feel of the voting portal would resemble that of Facebook, but the security would be far more stringent. For a discussion of security, see the section entitled "A Word on Technology".

A single page would show the top federal, provincial/state, and local issues being considered. You would be permitted to vote only once per issue. Periodically the top issues, as written and voted on by the people, would be tabled for a formal vote. Government employees would then write the proposed legislation, and put it forth for debate among the people. It would then be passed into law or rejected as determined by the people.

To prevent people from bogging the system down with numerous flippant ideas for legislation each person would be allowed only a few recommendations at each of the local, state/provincial, and federal levels each year.

Even before the first law is voted upon, a new constitution would be required to replace those that have become painfully anachronistic. As mentioned earlier, Iceland crowd sourced a new constitution replacing an old one that was created in the early 20th Century. Many of the countries of the Western world have constitutions much older than theirs.

The specific wording any proposed legislation would include the vote required for passage. 50% plus one would be the minimum, but often a two thirds majority would be recommended in the proposal. The actual requirements would be set forth in the constitution, charter, or other guiding document that has been agreed to in your jurisdiction.

To reiterate, a single screen on the voting portal would display the top ten or so items being considered for legislation at each of the three government levels. Another screen would show the present status of all current legislation being considered along with a tally of current voting results. Beside each pending bill would be a green light showing that the voting deadline is not imminent, yellow if the voting is due to close within the week, and red if the bill to be decided in the next 24 hours.

Old legislation would also be presented the same way. Bills that passed showing a green light, those that have been set aside temporarily with a yellow light, and those bills that were defeated with a red light.

New bills could not be substantively the same as anything considered in the last five years.

Now back to our example:

In another part of the country Marge is a shut in patient at a local hospital.

The Coming Age of Internetocracy

She is very civic minded and has studied every outstanding bill currently being considered, as well as every related document, both mandatory and optional. Even though she is elderly she is very adept at using a computer and the internet. If she wasn't she would've gone to a place specially set up to help her exercise her right to vote, perhaps the library down the street.

On the bills voted on by the surfer, she votes in the exact opposite opinion. No prison reform, yes on the speed limit law.

It's a stalemate. If only these two people vote, the bill will not pass.

A bill can only pass with a 50% plus one majority, if that is what is agreed upon in your jurisdiction. Others will set the bar at two-thirds, and so on. But in your area, it is 50% plus 1.

But wait, Josh has just logged in!

Josh is a wealthy businessman, very right-wing in his leanings.

After studying only the required documents, he votes "no" on prison reform, and "no" on lowering the speed limit to 60.

The "No" side wins.

The process has worked at the grassiest of the grassroots level!

Internetocracy has prevailed. The people have spoken.

The Beginning: A New Constitution

Our Mission

To empower each citizen to table and decide legislation by enabling them through social networking, personal broadcasting, and other internet technologies

facebook.com/INTERNETOCRACY

So, how did we get to this point (apart from a revolution that is)?

The point of a revolution is to bring about a powerful change; one that displaces all that existed before it.

In this case, the object of change is the constitution. An Internetocracy cannot exist in any industrialized nation today because their constitutions won't support it. That's because the constitution controls the system of government, the structure of government, and the very nature of voting.

One day a country will reach a point of creating a new constitution, as for example in Iceland where their early 20th Century constitution was replaced in 2011 with a new "crowd sourced" constitution whereby the citizens of that nation had direct input into its creation using the internet. It however was not a constitution that enabled Internetocracy, but the process is a harbinger of things to come.

When a new constitution is developed using the principles of Internetocracy it will have some marked differences from any constitution that exists today.

Like modern representative political systems (democracies, federations, republics, etc.) there will be variations, but all Internetocracy based constitutions will share one primary trait: they will enable citizens to directly table and decide legislation using social networking, personal broadcasting, and other tools of the internet.

Beyond that there could be great variation from one country to the next. One country could have an elected representative body that can table and decide legislation in parallel to the legislative body composed of the citizens. In such a scenario both legislative bodies would have to approve a bill for it to become law.

This is not the structure advocated in this book, but it is still a structure incorporating features of an Internetocracy.

A more favorable structure would be one where there are no elected representatives involved in the legislative process, nor are there any in the executive.

The executive consists of those people who will lead the various departments of the government, and the "chief" itself. We will return to this later in the chapter.

The Coming Age of Internetocracy

In our discussion of an appropriate constitution for an Internetocracy we will start with the legislative process, and we will focus on the federal level of government only.

The purpose of the constitution is not only to define the process of legislation, but also what safeguards are inherent in it to prevent a tyranny from arising.

In our form of government, where people at the lowest level are empowered, we must incorporate checks to the power of the majority over the minority.

Therefore there are two bodies in my vision of an Internetocracy. The first is the virtual "House of the People". This is the legislative body where each citizen is empowered to table and decide legislation, in a process described earlier in this book.

The House of the People is the only house with legislative capabilities. There is no Senate, etc. Furthermore, there is no executive or monarch empowered to veto the House of the People.

But how will the power of this people be kept in check so that it will not become tyrannical?

Structurally it will be checked by a body composed of minority interest groups. This body would have the power to review all bills and must approve them before they become law, but... they cannot totally veto new bills.

For discussion purposes we will call this the "Council of Special Interest Groups". They would consist of representatives from organizations such as the American Civil Liberties Union, Amnesty International, PETA, the Gay and Lesbian alliance, as well as the major religious groups and groups representing recognized visible minorities. The number of member organizations could be fixed at 100 to begin with and the membership decided by a public sector body.

If any member of the Council of Special Interest Groups does not approve a bill they send it back to the House of the People with recommendations. The House of the People considers the bill again and sends the revised bill back to the Council. The Council has one final opportunity to send the bill back to the House of the People for reconsideration. At this point the legislation, if approved by the House of the People becomes law with no further deliberation by the Council of Special Interests.

After a proposed law has passed through the review process performed by the Council of Special Interests, another important check is provided by the Judicial Branch of government who would review a law passed by the Legislative Branch to ensure that it complies with the constitution itself.

In an Internetocracy the Supreme Court justices would review every bill about to become law to ensure that the laws do not violate the rules of our very own constitution. The ultimate power always rests with the people however, since they can amend the constitution if the Justices initially ruled the law unconstitutional. This would however take time as the amendment to the constitution itself would have to be tabled, debated, and decided upon before the old bill is reintroduced (assuming the change to the Constitution was approved).

Remember that the Constitution would include a guarantee of rights and freedoms. If the proposed law violated one of these, there is a strong possibility that the people would not pass an amendment to change it, so the bill being considered above could be permanently defeated.

Once the legislation is approved by the Supreme Court Justices it becomes law and can never be challenged in a court of law on constitutional grounds.

Aside from the structural check, there are also two other important checks incorporated into the constitution that will provide safeguards to prevent a tyranny of the majority.

One of them is the hurdle to approve legislation. The bar could be set as low as 50% plus one, but that is not a definitive majority. To be definitive the bar should be placed at no less than two-thirds (i.e. 66.6%).

The more important safeguards are the rights and freedoms that will themselves be incorporated into the Constitution. Such rights as freedom of religion, freedom of speech, and the freedom of association would be embedded. Furthermore, it is likely in today's culture that the rights of the gay and lesbian community would be recognized (whereas they would not have been recognized in the days of our forefathers and foremothers).

This last point is important: social norms change over time. What is acceptable today is intolerable tomorrow. What is intolerable today may become acceptable tomorrow. Therefore a constitution should expire at some predetermined time, and be renegotiated by a later generation.

The Coming Age of Internetocracy

Thomas Jefferson was a great proponent of a constitution that expires. He believed that each generation should determine its own constitution. He suggested 19 years, but 30 to 50 years may be more appropriate.

If the constitution expired after a certain number of years, it will dissuade people from having an almost religious reverence for the document.

A constitution is not a religious document; it is a document that defines the government and its rights, as well as the fundamental freedoms of the people.

Now let us turn our attention to the executive.

The executive consists of those individuals hired by the people to run the various parts of the government. Note that I said "hired".

No one is elected in an Internetocracy, but people are hired to lead certain parts of the government.

The chief executive would be recruited by an executive search firm. Several candidates would be considered, their resumes exposed to public scrutiny, their salary requirements also exposed.

The executive search firm would make a recommendation, and so would the special advisers discussed earlier. Depending on the profile (in this case high, because we are talking about the chief), there would be many YouTube videos, blogs, tweets, etc.

In the end the people "hire" the individual and he or she is signed to a contract of say five years (which is also available for review by any citizen).

The Coming Age of Internetocracy

Just like any chief executive, the five year contract is not cast in stone. If the chief underperforms, the people can fire him or her at any point, subject to the terms of the contract of course.

The structure of our recommended government would look like this:

Federal Government in an Internetocracy

Legislative Branch of Government

Legislation tabled on-line by citizens

House of the People - based on principles of Internetocracy

Approval

Reviewed by Council of Minority Interests

Not Endorsed

Endorsed

Council of Minority Interests can ask for a law to be reconsidered by the House of the People (but only once)

Legislation decided on-line by citizens

Bill becomes Law

Executive Branch of Government

The head of state and federal departments are employees of the House of the People with No legislative or veto powers

Judicial Branch of Government

Supreme Court Justices are Employees of the House of the People with the power to render a law unconstitutional

By:
facebook.com/INTERNETOCRACY
A new political ideology

Notes:

1. Council of Minority Interest Groups: made up of representatives from 100 or so minority groups.
2. The members of the Executive and Judicial Branches are "hired and fired" by the House of the People.

In addition to the chief executive, the heads of other major government bodies (e.g. Health, Education, and Defence) as well as the Supreme Court Justices would also be hired and fired the same way … by the people.

The ultimate commander of the armed forces would be the chief executive hired by "we the people" for a period of five years. The chief executive would have no veto power over the legislation he or she is hired to facilitate.

Aside from the structure of government and a definition of rights and freedoms, a constitution supporting Internetocracy would also define the specific process of legislation.

How will a bill get tabled? Perhaps the five top trending issues are those which are tabled for resolution? Such mechanics could vary between countries, but as stated before: as long as citizens are directly empowered to table and decide legislation, the core requirement of an Internetocracy is fulfilled. It will most assuredly vary from country to country.

Another issue to be tackled in a constitution: should a citizen be required to pass a competency test to vote on an issue? In a true direct democracy the answer would be no, but Internetocracy is about empowering the individual to participate in the legislative process via the tools of the internet, not about enabling majority rule. This is how Internetocracy differs from electronic direct democracy; it is not about majority rule, it is about enabling the individual to participate in the legislative process.

To illustrate this important difference with a simple example:

Suppose that the matter being considered is this: Should the amount of new immigrants allowed into the country be increased from 100,000 to 200,000 per year? Seems like a simple question, but what if the country's majority opposed the increase? In a true electronic direct democracy the bill would be defeated. But that is not necessarily the case in an Internetocracy.

In an Internetocracy participation in the legislative process is voluntary, and on a per bill basis. Is everyone going to vote on every bill? No.

So in our example it's quite likely that the participation of the people who have recently immigrated, or who have relatives that want to immigrate, is going to be extremely high, whereas participation by the rest of the population could be quite low: many people will not care enough one way or another, so they will not participate. You are free to participate, but you are also free to not participate.

In this particular case, a true direct democracy would see the bill defeated (since the majority of citizens do not favor it), whereas the bill passes in an Internetocracy because the majority of *those participating* is in favor of it.

So in an Internetocracy, requiring citizens to prove their capability to vote on an issue is acceptable (but not required). Two different countries can each adopt two different policies (one with testing, the other without), and still be considered Internetocracies.

To reiterate: the main difference between a true direct democracy and Internetocracy is the nature of the body voting on any issue. In an Internetocracy the majority does not necessarily rule (as it would in a direct democracy), but rather the majority of stake holders who have made themselves available to vote on a particular issue.

So an Internetocracy begins when a new constitution is born.

The price of apathy towards public affairs is to be ruled by evil men

Plato

(Ancient Greek Philosopher He was the world's most influential philosopher. 428 BC-348 BC)

A message from facebook.com/INTERNETOCRACY
Visit our page to learn about a new political ideology (and "Like" if you are interested)

Change by Peaceful Means

Gandhi and other intellectuals have promoted a peaceful path to change. Although such means have had some success, they are by far the minority.

There will at first be peaceful attempts at change aside those who are more radical and less patient.

But as the power center resists the change, the growing frustration of the populace will see the support for those who promote violent change gain in popularity, especially among the young male population.

The police response to the Occupy Movement exemplifies the above statement. In an article by Naomi Wolf published in the Nov 25th 2011 issue of the Guardian (UK) "There is a coordinated effort to use violence on the Occupy Movement because it threatens the personal congressional profit streams of elected representatives."

The longer that legitimate calls for change are resisted, the stronger and more virulent the agents of change will become.

Until one day they take up arms.

This is not an endorsement of violence. The most constructive course for this to take is for representative political systems to re-invent themselves into Internetocracies so that long-term economic grow can be sustained. This is possible and preferred, but it has not been the way that changes such as this have taken hold in the past. We can remain optimistic, however.

Since no large corporation or wealthy individuals benefit from our vision, social networking is the primary method by which the vision of Internetocracy is spread.

The sentiments of Joshua Barnes, writing on the Internetocracy Facebook page sum it up very nice "it sounds like it [Internetocracy] would work but first we have to take the power from those who benefit from our suffering. That is going to be the hard part because they won't give in easily or peacefully."

The Arguments Against

There are many who would argue that the average person cannot vote directly on an issue, and that they need to be represented by better qualified people.

I argue that most of the "qualified" people tend to be those who wish to use an elected position to consolidate a position of power for them self. Such people are inherently motivated by selfish reasons are poor representatives, especially when the populace has the means (the Internet) to study issues and represent themselves on each individual issue they feel strongly about.

The system of decision making has not changed significantly in many generations.
The internet is now embedded thoroughly in every aspect of our culture other than political decision making.

lets change that.

facebook.com/Internetocracy

Today's elected law making representatives would be replaced with elected officials who would serve as advisers to their constituents. They would not decide the fate of new bills. They just provide expert advice to their constituents and allow the masses to decide for themselves.

There are also those who would argue that technology can be manipulated. Those were probably the same voices that alleged that internet banking was not possible because the internet could never be secure enough to manipulate wealth. That, of course, has proven to be untrue.

By way of comparison, if billions of dollars can be moved around daily on the internet, the medium is secure enough to facilitate direct voting on new legislation at the grass roots level.

A number of specific criticisms will be examined later in this book.

Ghost Towns

The centers of power will not in fact be ghost towns, but the buildings that house the people who represent constituents will be largely empty. These building are no longer the primary center for debate. Debate is waged on social networking sites, YouTube, and a variety of other forums.

Consequently there will be no need for a congress, a parliament, or a duma. The process is "virtual".

But there will be one aspect of government that will be exempt from significant change: the actual civil servants who are employed by government to run the day-to-day affairs of the government.

A new level of civil servant will also be added: those who administer the voting portal, and those who translate the results of voting into action. There will also be civil servants who help write the official bills tabled for consideration on the voting portal.

The "Executive" powers will no longer be held by elected representatives. These functions will be carried out by people hired and fired via the Internetocracy. Positions such as the "Chief Executive" of the government, "Chief of Education", and "Chief of Health" will all fit into such a category.

An Executive search firm will search for several candidates and place their credential and salary requirements on the web for all to see. Then "we the people" will hire one of them, and when the time comes "we the people" will fire them. Terminating their contract will be handled according to a term in their employment contract. The contract could be for five years, but we the people can fire them at any time. After five years the contract is renegotiated and the people decide to approve the new contract (or whether a new candidate should be searched for). Great "chiefs" could be on the job for many, many years. Poor ones could be ousted in less than a year.

And they will carry out exactly what we the voters decide, or they will be ousted.

Political appointments would cease to exist. Ambassadors and judges would be recruited by executive search firms, and would go through a normal hiring process administered by the public sector.

In time of war, the defence of the country would be the responsibility of the "Chief Executive", whose job duties would include that of "commander and chief" of the country. He or she would report directly to the people, but the military will report directly to him (or her). A declaration of war would require an endorsement by the people on the voting portal. If the people concur, wars of aggression would cease to exist. A new constitution, crowd sourced (as has been recently done in Iceland) could make it illegal.

I conclude this section with comments posted on Facebook/Internetocracy by a few of its users:

"I have been saying this for a long time. The old representative form of government is out dated and it is too easy to corrupt. I don't need anyone to represent me. I can think for myself." - Kerry McCauley

A More Formal Description

Summary

Internetocracy is a political concept based on the premise that advancements in internet technology should be utilized to create a more direct political system. This is a concept for a completely different form of government than anything currently in place in the world. It is a vision of a new political system, not a new political party working within any present political system.

In this paradigm, there is no longer a reliance on an elected representative government, but a reliance on each constituent to decide the fate of any legislation they feel compelled to participate on deciding.

Representatives are replaced with special advisers whose job is to use their expertise to advise and advocate for their constituents, especially when the legislation is complex.

Background

The concept of elected representative government is a paradigm that has its roots in a time when communication, technology, and the level of education necessitated such a model.

Over time certain regions of the world have become more literate, communication has been greatly improved, and internet technology has become widespread and secure. Consequently, it is argued that the population of such regions can and should exercise a more direct influence in the law making process through the use of a secure internet based system.

The Coming Age of Internetocracy

"The quintessential question is can democracy survive the internet? I don't think so. At least not if it continues to operate in its current form" - Internetocracy: Political Reform by Way of Technology - (published by Getontheboat.wordpress.com).

The Vision

The vision of Internetocracy is to facilitate the direct participation of citizens in the lawmaking process through a system of a secure internet-enabled political system with special members of the community advising and mentoring small groups of the citizenry (but not deciding legislation on their behalf), legal protection for the rights of minorities, constraints to make it difficult to consolidate political power, and an emphasis on social networking applications to link people together.   We are the law makers!   We make the decisions!

Internetocracy is a political system adaptable to a democratic republic, a constitutional monarchy, a confederation, etc.

The fundamental unit for enacting legislation is the person. The fundamental unit for electing advisers is the community.

The chief difference between this system and the current system is that an elected official cannot vote on any legislation. The ultimate decisions are made directly by the citizens over a secure encrypted connection.

Mission:

1. Harness the power of the internet as a secure legislative tool, particularly the social networking platforms.

2. Create a political system where the people can propose new bills and each person can vote on any bill they have a stake in according to their conscience (with the aide, wisdom, and council of an adviser they respect).
3. Retain expertise to advise and mentor the electorate.
4. Make it difficult for any individual to consolidate political power.
5. Protect minorities.

Benefits

The ability for each voter to participate directly in the law making process pushes the process down to its lower level, and reduces the reliance on a concentrated group of people who may be tempted to use such power for personal gain, or who may be easy targets for people who wish to compromise the process.

It is argued that in an Internetocracy, it is more difficult for a small group of people with interests in opposition to the mass population to unduly influence the process for their own benefit to the detriment of the constituency as a whole.

Another potential benefit is that more people are apt to vote if they can do so from the comfort of their own home on their own computer.   This is particular true of people who may not be very mobile due to illness or who are frail.

The Coming Age of Internetocracy

The diagram below shows the current state of representative political systems ("the world today") contrasted with tomorrow's world of Internetocracy.

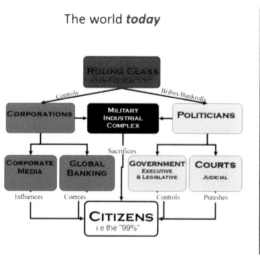

Visit facebook.com/internetocracy If you are interested, "Like" us

Federal Voting Regions

With a system where representatives are no longer required to decide the fate of bills, the entire system of geographic representation at the federal level becomes redundant. Not only is a congressman from Rhode Island not required, the idea of Rhode Island being represented is not necessarily required. Perhaps the one useful vestige of this concept is that an expert adviser could be a resident of this area to more easily provide face-to-face interaction with his constituents.

Each voting citizen of Rhode Island would cast a vote, and those votes would be tabulated against the votes of the entire nation. In such a system a law cannot pass unless the popular vote was more than two thirds of the total.

In a Commonwealth country like Canada there would no longer be ridings, because there is no need to send a representative from a distant region to the center of political decision making. Through the use of our internet portal, we are all at the center of political decision making.

Because the process is virtual the special adviser at the federal level could spend more time in his constituency providing face-to-face interaction.

A Word on Political Leadership

We don't need to elect a new president, or a new prime minister, or a new political party. We don't need to elect ministers, congressmen, senators or any other type of position that votes on behalf of hundreds of thousands or even millions of people. We need to throw out the entire representative system and build something new that is not so easy for a "ruling class" to corrupt.

We still need leaders, however, but they will take on a different role and become far more numerous because they will be precluded from representing massive groups and will instead represent a far smaller local group of no more than 1000 citizens.

In fact, a citizen can more easily "elect" an adviser than in the current paradigm because the ramifications are not so great as to warrant a formal highly controlled election process. The citizen will "elect" their adviser by simply selecting one of the many persons offering to act in such a capacity in their district with a single mouse click. There will be several of these leader/advisers in a region who could conceivably work together and convene regular town hall meetings to discuss matters. Furthermore the constituent can easily switch to another adviser at any time with one mouse click.

Not only will the adviser/leaders be unable to consolidate significant power due to the limited amount of people they advise, but their remuneration will be such that only those who are at or near the 1000 person base limit will be able to earn a stipend from the function large enough to make a living on (and not an exorbitant living). But they will be able to do the job full-time.

The Coming Age of Internetocracy

The best adviser/mentors will have 1000 people in their group, and will also have a wait list for those wishing to get on their list.   In the mean time those on the wait list must use a different adviser/mentor.

Despite having selected a certain person as your adviser/mentor, there is nothing to stop you from reading the recommendations and other information supplied by any other adviser/mentor, or anyone in the world for that matter.

If you are a Noam Chomsky fan, you will be free to adhere to his recommendations concerning certain pending legislation. If you think that the recommendations by a Greenpeace are the way to go, that is your choice.   If your Baptist minister recommends voting a certain way on a bill and you agree, you can vote according to those recommendations. But your adviser/mentor is just that, a person you have selected from among a local group offering to act in such a capacity. Your election was performed with a single mouse click and can be changed at any time.

I close this section with a quote from Micah Sifry: "Going from a world of top-down leaders who use hierarchy, secrecy and spin to conduct their business to a leader-full world filled with self-starting network weavers who are transparent and accountable about their actions will take some getting used to ..... [Occupy Wall Street] represents the flowering of something very deep about our networked age. It is personal democracy in action, where everyone plays a role in shaping the decisions that affect our lives." – Micah Sifry, "How technology is reorganizing political protest movements", CNN.com Nov. 14, 2011

Moderate and Modified Versions

If those in power voluntarily gave much of that power up, it would be possible to modify the current political landscape to allow the direct participation of the masses via the internet.

In this paradigm, the elected official no longer votes on laws. His or her purpose is to see to it that the will of the constituent, as reflected through direct voting on each proposed law in the voting portal, is carried out by government. It is, as has been stated before, also an advisory role. Thus the elected official would be a person with significant credentials.

The representative would be elected, but not to make laws. He or she could also be impeached by the electorate and removed from office if the constituents feel that performance has been unsatisfactory.

The previous descriptions for how direct voting by the masses would take place in the voting portal all still apply, as do the examples. It is just the role of the current politician that has changed.

The key point is that elected officials would no longer be "law makers", they would be agents of their constituents empowered to ensure that their will as expressed directly in the voting portal is carried out and to assist them.

Because the representative does not have the ability to decide the fate of new bills, the power of the corporate lobbyist would become negligible as they no longer have just one person to influence from a constituency. They essentially have to influence *every* constituent. It will be far more onerous to attempt to influence thousands where previously only one person had to be influenced.

Another variant on Internetocracy would allow constituents to assign all of their voting power to another individual or assign their vote on specific bills to different individuals. They could assign all of their voting power, or just part of it, bill by bill.

This is not a variation that I personally condone. The ability to coerce individuals to assign their vote is too great a threat. By keeping the voting power fragmented there is little risk of coercion as each person wields little power. The power resides in the whole of the electorate.

Criticism and Rebuttal

Like any new system there are many detractors with criticisms that are sometimes valid. Here are some of those criticisms with a rebuttal to them.

Criticism: The internet is not secure enough to facilitate Internetocracy.

Rebuttal: The security embedded in certain aspects of internet traffic is encrypted and now considered very safe. As a primary example I cite the banking industry. Billions of dollars are transacted safely and securely over the internet every day. Most readers will be very familiar with this.

Criticism: Technology is too vulnerable to natural disasters, power outages, computer virus' and hacking.

Rebuttal: power outages and natural disasters are a threat to any political system. Furthermore, when such events occur, it is the day-to-day functioning of government that is most disrupted.   Legislation is a long process and it is unlikely that all but a lengthy outage would have any meaningful effect.

Computer virus' and hacking are also a threat, but no more so than they would be for online services that you depend on such as banking.

Criticism: Internetocracy can be hi-jacked by people who are the experts in the code used.

Rebuttal: Again I point to the banking system where trillions of dollars are at risk if internal and external controls were more permissive than they are. However, on-line banking is very secure because of these controls and it has been in use for several years now. The internet programs that support the political process would be at least as secure as those in the banking industry.

The technology to vote online is also a paradigm that people have to get used to, just like on-line purchasing. Think of the initial trepidation people had when the concept of buying things on-line first emerged. Ten years later the security of on-line commerce became almost taken for granted by the consumer.

There was a time **when some people were afraid to buy things on the internet.**
There was a time **when some people were afraid to do their banking on the internet**
This is a time **when some people are afraid....**
to allow **direct citizen participation in the legislative process on the internet.**

Times change, don't they?

Some thoughts from facebook.com/INTERNETOCRACY

A new political system for the next generation.

In the words of Jt Chiaruttini, a user of the Internetocracy Facebook page: "as far as security issues go.....it would be a big political football and the "establishment" would most certainly use it to discourage the idea but it really wouldn't be as a big of a concern as one might think. If you have ever read the book "Freakonomics" or seen the movie, when working with large numbers like the population of the US the ability to manipulate this would be severely limited by polling and verification samples. I think you would be able to ascertain with a high degree of certainty whether voting was legit."

Criticism: Internetocracy will not support my view of the world. Case in point, it may not result in the legalization of marijuana, or it may not abolish the death penalty.

<u>Rebuttal</u>: The political process should not pander to a minority interest group so long as that groups human rights are not violated. The rule of the majority of those who chose to participate is a basic tenet of Internetocracy.

<u>Criticism</u>: A tyranny of the majority over the minority would ensue if Internetocracy was in use.

<u>Rebuttal</u>: The unproven notion that a political system rooted in direct democracy will become a tyranny over the minority has been challenged in recent years. In the book ***The Logic of Collective Action: Public Goods and the Theory of Groups*** by Mancur Olson, Jr. (first published in 1965 by the Harvard University Press) Mr. Olson maintains that large groups will face relatively high costs when attempting to organize for collective action while small groups will face relatively low costs. Furthermore, individuals in large groups will gain less per capita of successful collective action; individuals in small groups will gain more per capita through successful collective action. Hence, in the absence of selective incentives, the incentive for group action diminishes as group size increases, so that large groups are less able to act in their common interest than small ones.

The book concludes that, not only will collective action by large groups be difficult to achieve even when they have interests in common, but situations could also occur where the minority (bound together by concentrated selective incentives) can dominate the majority.

That being said, it is imperative that some sort of bill of rights and freedoms be in place upon which all legislation must abide in a world of Internetocracy to ensure that the majority do not infringe upon the rights and freedoms of the minority through legislation. An example of this would be protecting the rights of the gay and lesbian community to coexist peacefully and free of discrimination.

Not to diminish the arguments above that Internetocracy will not result in a tyranny of the minority, I further say that there is clear evidence that we now have a situation where a small "ruling class" clearly controls the political and economic landscape which is a form of tyranny of minority over a the majority. This form of tyranny is rampant in any country whose political structure is representative in nature.

Criticism: The masses are not educated or intelligent enough to decide upon legislation.

Rebuttal: While the electorate may not be as educated or intelligent on a whole as those who are in power today, they are far more educated than the masses of most first world nations were when most representative political systems were first set up.

There would also be very capable men and women of wisdom hired to advise their constituents and make recommendations. A "brain trust" will continue to exert influence, but they will be far less open to corrupting influences and will be forced to stay closely in touch with their constituents. In complex matters they will be the ones upon who the electorate rely upon for guidance and wisdom as they make the final decision.

In the words of one of the fans of Internetocracy "to help educate individual voters who are not computer savvy there could be TV channels, one for each issue, showing mini seminars on that issue. These could be done by the advisers in a format like any business presentation including charts and/or graphs. Instead of putting computers in all homes how about using libraries? They already all have computers with internet they would just have to be expanded and possibly staffed by individuals who work for the office of the special adviser as their trained and fully informed designee. "

Yet another suggestion from a fan of Internetocracy: there could be "free classes to teach people how to use the internet. There are libraries that have computers available and there could be more sites made available for free. Starbucks has internet connections, maybe they could set up a few machines for those who come there w/o their own. Always remember, our privacy has been taken from us, our govt. can listen on our phone lines, use what we think as private information, they are in our lives in EVERYTHNG. We need a government, but we need a govt. that really DOES work for the people. "

From yet another follower "Educate school children about their rights and responsibilities as citizens and teach them how this system works. In a couple of generations it will have transitioned to something not plagued by citizens who are politically ignorant and asleep at the wheel."

Ryan Sonak envisions a "huge outbreak of citizen's videos on YouTube trying to sway public opinion. You would not need very much money to get people to listen to your ideas, like politicians do now. Certain people will gain respect and popularity by creating trends in topics and the public will most likely jump on the bandwagon with people they see making good points/proposals. I think this is a great idea, everyone can be involved, and it should eventually educate us so much that we will all have a new understanding on how the world works and should be ran. There will be some problems, of course, but I believe that the majority of the people will make the right decisions. Anger will probably be frowned upon by the majority and education will control the outcome of every vote."

Criticism: Representative political decision making amounts to a delegation of law making which frees the masses to carry out their day-to-day business. In other words, the legislative process is too time-consuming.

Rebuttal: This is also a valid concern. The process will have to facilitate giving the electorate an overview of all pending legislation and allowing them to pick and choose which bills they wish to participate on. As shown earlier in this book, most people will only want to participate on deciding bills which have a direct influence on their lives or over which they feel strongly about. Few people will vote on everything.

Furthermore the bills will have to be presented with easy to understand summaries of the legislation along with the recommendation of the special adviser. Such information would likely be mandatory before someone could log a vote. From this point the voter could study more materials, view more YouTube videos, and discuss with other voters before ultimately deciding the issue. The voter would be free to choose to ignore the recommendation of the special adviser and vote with his or her conscience.

<u>Criticism</u>: Not everyone has a computer or the internet.

<u>Rebuttal</u>: the use of personal computers, smart phones, and the internet is wide spread through the first world. Still there are those that do not have access to these resources. The government would have to create a grants system to ensure that even the poorest have access to at least one computer in the household with an internet connection. This should be as basic as the right to a primary education.

In cases where people are not comfortable with the use of a computer, there must be centers where they can find both a computer and someone to aid them so that they can participate in the political process.

In the words of one Internetocracy fan "You could have set locations where people who do not have the internet could go to learn to use the system. [Perhaps they] have to pass a negotiated test in order to be eligible.... for everyone not just these people), register, and vote... like a public city building set up with a bunch of computers. This overall idea would make it to where you have to be educated to vote. And I like the 66% idea."

Yet another fan envisions town "voting cafes". "Current home/commercial construction designs usually include basic electric- and phone-line access. Perhaps in the future, installation of some sort of computer device that allows services for voting, getting emergency help, etc. could be a common feature in building design."

<u>Criticism</u>: The advisers could still be unduly influenced by lobbyists and then present a spin to the facts of an issue that is not in the interests of the common good.

<u>Rebuttal</u>: Once again, this is a valid concern.   The need to have men and women of wisdom guiding the rest of the electorate unfortunately puts them in a position of power and influence.   The fact that they do not vote on behalf of their constituents lessens this risk that they have been unduly influenced to what I propose is an acceptable level.

Furthermore, keeping their constituency as small as possible will make this risk negligible.   One special adviser per 1000 people would allow the adviser to personally know much of the constituency, but yet not have a consolidation of power that would not warrant any special interest in their ability to influence.

The "Perfect Storm"

Currently we have two developments that are about to come together: The internet has evolved to allow direct voting on bills, and there is intense dissatisfaction with the existing political system.

The intense dissatisfaction stems from the constituents perception that professional politicians are in fact working for the wealthiest individuals or for corporations. In other words, politicians are seen as using their positions of power to benefit themselves and not for the good of the people. This is a generalization of course, but this is the way the masses currently perceive politicians.

The "Occupy" Movement

The first version of this document was published shortly before a worldwide phenomenon erupted.... the so called "Occupy" movement. It began with "Occupy Wall Street" and has since spread to many cities around the world.

According to CNN Author Alan Silverleib in an article published on that website (Oct. 18, 2011) called Occupy Wall Street: How Long Can It Last?:

"While the protesters highlighted a number of causes, the overarching theme remained the same: populist anger over an out-of-touch corporate, financial and political elite."

I propose this is the beginning of a movement that will eventually lead to a revised system of politics, one that is *direct* with its defining characteristic the complete absence of representative law makers.... a movement henceforth known as "Internetocracy".

In an article written by Fordham University communications professor Paul Levinson in the Christian Science Monitor (Oct. 25, 2011) called "Does 'Occupy Wall Street have leaders? Does it need any?", the Occupy Wall Street [movement] and similar movements, symbolize another rise of direct democracy where people collectively make decisions for themselves without having elected leaders that has not actually been seen since ancient times.

The link between Internetocracy and the Occupy Movement are best exemplified by the words of Diana Strait: "So I'm not the only one with this "radical" idea

[Internetocracy]. That makes me feel a little less radical. But still, how do we get this change accomplished? I'm in week 4 now, marching down the street holding a sign and getting both negative and positive remarks but still no change in sight."

Musings of the Author

- Aside from casting off the representative concept Internetocracy is ideologically neutral. It is entirely dependent on the ideological leanings of the majority of people who vote. If they have socialist leanings the style of government will resemble a socialist one. If the electorate is conservative in its leanings, the government will lean that way.
- Attempts to launch an Internetocracy within a representative system are doomed to fail. In such a system the people will always be marginalized because the representative parties, with their ability to concentrate power, will be able to summon vast resources from those who wish to concentrate that power.
- A distinct set of definitions for the word *republic* evolved in the United States. In common parlance a republic is a state that does not practice direct democracy but rather has a government indirectly controlled by the people. This is known as representative democracy. This understanding of the term was originally developed by James Madison, and notably employed in Federalist Paper No. 10. This meaning was widely adopted early in the history of the United States, including in Noah Webster's dictionary of 1828. It was a novel meaning to the term; representative democracy was not an idea mentioned by Machiavelli and did not exist in the classical republics.
  William R. Everdell. *The End of Kings: A History of Republics and Republicans.* University of Chicago Press, 2000. pg. 6

- We presently live in a tyranny, where the minority (i.e. the "1%") exploits the majority. Some have argued that Internetocracy might lead to a tyranny of the majority over the minority. One of the core principles of our movement is that precautions must be taken to ensure that this does not happen. The place to do that is in a constitution or a bill of rights and freedoms. Such documents are the starting point in creating an Internetocracy and assuring the rights of visible minorities, freedom of religion, and the elimination of discrimination based on sexual preference. Tolerance, peace, responsibility, transparency, and accountability ... these are some of our core values.
- The legislative process in an Internetocracy is organic, moving as fast as any problem could. Only the internet can support the rapid decision making required in today's world.

Musings by Others

The comments below are from the users of facebook.com/Internetocracy:

- Jackie Warren Demijohn - With the internet, we should be able to vote from the comfort of our laptop. And if this is true, then we do not need "representatives" in our capitols to make our decisions, we can all vote on it together.
- From Marc Train - Straw poll to gauge interest in whether or not an issue is worth putting into the hopper. General discussion is opened up to discuss various solutions and ideas. Straw poll taken again on the ideas that seem 'strongest'. Then you move into formalizing the 'language' of the strongest idea, and from there it becomes an official vote.
- Emily Anderson: This is a fascinating and brilliant idea...Probably inevitable in the post humanist age.
- Brandon Joubert: There need be no elections. The society defines the criteria for a person to qualify as an elder or person of integrity. These elders or qualifying ones then form cells at each community level of which there is no leader, just a body of qualified people. These bodies choose members to form part of the regional governing bodies, and these bodies choose members to form part of the global governing body. In order to be effective there needs to be a written code to which the bodies subject themselves. This is the area of weakness because man has proven his inability to control his own steps - so any written code originating from man is doomed to fail. With an effective written code, tiers of governing bodies it

would be possible to establish a global government that supersedes nationality, race and ethnicity.

- Kerry McCauley - Internetocracy is an idea whose time has come. I don't need a politician representing me. Politicians are all bought and paid for. Our liberties have been infringed on and the system is broke. I have been saying this for years, and the internet is the answer.
- Benjamin Hamilton - In a lot of ways, I've viewed the Occupy movement as the first real step moving human culture toward a more direct form of democracy, albeit tentatively and blindly at the moment. I think that it's inevitable and unstoppable; much as no amount of trying could stop the adoption of the printed word or representational forms of democracy, it's simply the most logical, liberating, and efficient way to organize people.
- Jc Skues - Our Thomas Paine just published his common sense for the I pad generation of people's politics. We're liberated.

About the Author

Lawrence Compagna is a management and information technology consultant who advises large public sector organizations on how to streamline both their processes and their information technology infrastructure to achieve greater efficiency and be more effective.

He resides in Southern California.

Correspondence can be sent to:

Box 437, 24 Roy Street, Seattle Washington. 98109

http://www.facebook.com/Internetocracy